# Squirrelland

# SQUIRRELLAND

## IMAGINATION
### AND THE
## ALASKA RED SQUIRREL

BY ERIC WADE
& PHOTOGRAPHY BY DOYLANNE WADE

SHANTI ARTS PUBLISHING
BRUNSWICK, MAINE

Published by Shanti Arts Publishing

Designed by Shanti Arts Designs

All photographs are by Doylanne Wade
and are used with her permission.

Shanti Arts LLC
193 Hillside Road
Brunswick, Maine 04011
shantiarts.com

Printed in the United States of America

ISBN: 978-1-962082-01-3 (print; softcover)
ISBN: 978-1-962082-05-1 (e-book)

Library of Congress Control Number: 2023945457

*To our friends on the rivers and in the woods
who have helped us along the way.*

# CONTENTS

# ACKNOWLEDGMENTS

Many people helped me with *Squirrelland*. James Wade read the earliest draft and offered insights and ideas. He read it again near its completion and suggested ways I might consider bringing it to an end. Jack Wade, Jed wade, and Jake Wade shared memories and stories and encouraged me to complete the project. Jake Haugland suggested ideas for pulling the observation data together that was immensely helpful. Helen Riley, Jon Holmgren, and Jack Evans shared squirrel stories. Holly Schaaf and Emma Rademacher provided the inspiration to replicate a squirrel study at the cabin. Sarah Birdsall, John Harvey, Chris Lundgren, and Deb Vanasse read and commented on the final version. Their thoughts are included here. I am deeply indebted to publisher Christine Cote. And Doylanne Wade, who's always been my wilderness partner, provided the gorgeous photography. Her tenacious attitude toward getting the shot is admirable and effective. She also read throughout the process, influencing every page.

The way to our little cabin, our home for two months of the year.

# INTRODUCTION

We're fascinated with bigness. Big brains, boats, businesses, behaviors, bulletins, bullies, and billionaires dominate the headlines and overwhelm us—many more Bs could be added to this list. If it's big, it's important. We view the natural world similarly. The animals that capture our imagination and receive the most attention are the big ones. The most common question after a return from the woods of interior Alaska is: "Did you see any bears?" followed by wolves and moose. I've never had anyone ask me: "Did you see any squirrels?" I've noticed something, though. After more than forty years venturing into the north woods: most animals are small. The big are few and far between.

Some have suggested that this captivation with all that is massive has become destructive. I agree. We learn from a young age that only large is special, and only the giants among us are worthy of the best, but obviously that is nonsense. Take the small from the world, and the big will vanish; the converse is not true.

•

A child's birthday party, a daisy along the road, a cloud that was sure to get us wet, it didn't matter. Doylanne always rushed for the camera. For most of our fifty years together, she didn't have the photography equipment to produce the quality she hoped for, but still the memories were captured, experience gained, and we have hundreds of those stored in boxes, some we know where they are, most we've forgotten and sometimes now find with surprise and delight. I recently rummaged through a storage shed looking for something to throw away because we have accumulated far too much stuff, as is what happens if you never discard anything, and during my search I discovered a packet of photos that chronicled a trip she and I made to Yellowstone in the early 1970s. One of the photos was unexpected; I held a pretty dang nice rainbow trout, which I'd forgotten all about until that moment, then it all came back to me, and I relived a very special journey we took to the mountains years ago.

That's what you will find here. She has spent decades recording our numerous adventures in Alaska's wilderness. Her photos have appeared in *Cabin: An Alaska Wilderness Dream* and *Upstream: In the Alaska Wilderness,* as well as *Alaska Magazine.*

We hope you enjoy this journey to our homestead in Alaska's interior and our observations in Squirrelland.

# PART I

After long hours on the river, we look for a place to camp.
Sometimes it's just too pretty to stop.

# ONE

# LET'S IMAGINE

*The wolf exerts a powerful influence on the human imagination. It takes your stare and turns it back on you.*

—Barry Lopez, *Of Wolves and Men*

I've only seen a handful of wolves in the wild, all sightings along a river—the lone wolf loping on a beach or a pack lounging in the sun. So what I know about wolves is a mixture of reading, a few sightings, and my imagination, for I've never followed one in the woods to study it for myself. The same is true for all animals. I've watched many moose blend silently into the trees, huge animals that disappear instantly like pale smoke. Once they fade from sight, I can only imagine what they do.

Imagining is what I must do as well as I follow the wanderings of the red squirrel in this book. I ask that you go along with me on a short journey. By mixing our experiences with squirrels, both wild and urban, with the work of researchers and our imaginations, we can together consider the North American red squirrel in the wilderness of interior Alaska.

Let's imagine a North America red squirrel running along a gnarled spruce branch, a slalom route taken many times before, its movement unique among other tree dwellers, its explosiveness eye blinking. It leaps to a higher branch and stops in a heartbeat. It wastes no energy, every twitch purposeful. With its head rock-still, it can scan the surroundings with excellent color vision. Its pale-yellow lenses function much like sunglasses. It can focus across the retina, meaning it processes superb vision out the sides of its eyes. Humans have peripheral vision, but with a marred, out of focus image, whereas, a red squirrel can clearly see the designs of a fluttering butterfly off to its side without moving its head.

Always clean and well-groomed, poised for action.

The squirrel appears to be weightless. It bounds into the autumn air to another branch and runs to the spruce tips and balances there on the slender ends, hind feet gripping the waving and bouncing boughs. A nine-ounce, diminutive super athlete, all muscle, speed, and agility, masters the high-bar of the wilderness, the wobbly tip of a white spruce. At birth it weighed half an ounce, a helpless, hairless peanut with little chance to ever leave the nest. Its eyes stay closed for nearly a month.

This squirrel is from the order **Rodentia**, family **Sciuridae**, and its scientific name is **Tamiasciurus hudsonicus**. It's the only squirrel I've seen at our place in the boreal forest in interior Alaska, but there is another. Flying squirrels also live in the trees here, but after years poking around in the woods, I've never seen one, so I'll let them be and focus only on the *hudsonicus*. I've seen dozens of them through the years, dashing through horsetail and rose bushes to tree trunks, dodging spruce grouse along the way.

My imaginary squirrel picks its way to a dense growth of spruce cones and begins biting through the soft stems and tossing the cones to the ground, sometimes in clusters of three or four, each landing with a soft thud near the base of the tree, a unique sound in the forest. As it jerks its head to toss the cones, the hair on its head is illuminated by a ray of sunlight, revealing the color that explains its name, a burnt red, warm, earthy color.

Its belly is white, as are the circles around each eye. Its tail, often stretched for balance, is tipped with dense gray and black hairs. These tail hairs have bands of color, meaning a strand of hair has different colors. I haven't noticed much variation in the coloring of red squirrels. They all look about the same to me, donned in a rich coat with a remarkable ability to disappear in a shadow. They do, though, appear in different sizes. Young squirrels, not long out of the nest, look like little adults.

After throwing a dozen clusters from the tree, the squirrel descends, again dashing, jumping, and freezing in its steps. On the ground now with the cones at its

feet, it pauses to eat one. Above the tree canopy, a bald eagle catches a thermal beneath a cumulus cloud and soars, turning, dipping, and radically climbing and most certainly looking for something to eat. The squirrel, now on its haunches, holds a cone in its hands and pulls away the scales (also called bracts) with its incisors, eating the seeds beneath. Its fourth finger, commonly referred to as the ring finger by humans, is its longest, presumably the extra length helpful while gripping branches. Soon a small pile of spruce scales form at its feet. It grabs a band of cones and darts to a midden at the base of a spruce. The eagle, soon to become a dot in the blue, follows the cumulus into the distance.

With danger momentarily absent, the squirrel sings, yes sings. I've never heard a squirrel sing but can imagine it. A story passed down by distant ancestors in southwest Alaska tells the story of a squirrel (it could have been a red squirrel) that sings to a raven blocking access to its den. The raven begins to dance to the squirrel's song, and the squirrel slips inside. This story is recounted in a remarkable book, *Nunakun-gguq Ciutengqertut, They Say They Have Ears Through the Ground: Animal Essays from Southwest Alaska.*


My wife, Doylanne, and I near the end of five weeks at our homestead watching squirrels, doing our best to extend our stay to the last days before the river turns sluggish with ice, and we must head to town. We closely watch the river and clouds, while frozen leaves fall upon us, colorful leaves heavily falling like Newton's apple to the hardening earth.

Thousands of leaves blanket our yard. A single large deciduous tree might have more than thirty thousand of them, and here along a stretch of river between Denali and the Yukon River, trees stand thick as bristles on a brush. Under a thick canopy of paper birch, yellow and russet leaves fall together in the cold.

We'll soon depart for town where we'll spend the winter, but the river, clouds, dead leaves, and noisy red squirrels will stay.

# TWO

# SQUIRRELS IN LITERATURE

*The clearest way into the Universe is through a forest wilderness.*
—John Muir, *John of the Mountains*

We waited too long at the homestead that autumn, and our trip home proved among the most difficult we'd ever experienced. Ice rapidly formed on the river, and the outboard quit midway to the launch.

The day before, the river ran cold steel, and the world glowed golden. A late September storm caught us ill-prepared.

All turned cold without warning.

We spent five days on the river, drifting, constantly attempting repair, and eventually camping each evening when darkness made travel dangerous. Finally at our home near Wasilla, thermostat set at seventy degrees, early winter descended on us like an avian predator, squeezing us to near asphyxiation.

I thought of our small red squirrel neighbors and began looking for books about them, finding dozens of children's stories with a squirrel protagonist, but there was not as much written about the squirrel's life and behavior as I thought there would be, certainly not compared to the big animals like bears, wolves, and moose.

It's important to understand, as best we can, the lacing fingers of humanity and the animal kingdom. Writers and researchers who focus on animals other that *Homo sapiens*, in my humble opinion, are among our most valued—even those who study squirrels. Although squirrels are not at the top of ethologists' lists and are often justifiably maligned by humankind, they are unquestionably vital. They live in the trees, underground, and can fly—well sort of. They prosper in the wilderness and in urban environments; they are survivors. Squirrels, I believe, are much more valuable than we know.

During my reading, I discovered a study of Eastern gray squirrels in the Boston Common Central Burying Ground. Truly well written and thorough, and I add this in admiration: simple in design. The article inspired me to replicate the study on wild red squirrels in the Alaska wilderness, a project that seemed like a fun idea that would take up any idle time I might find myself with at the homestead. I set out then to gain insight on the status of the red squirrel in the hierarchy of the boreal forest animal kingdom.

I found the author of the study online and learned that she wasn't a scientist at all, but a junior at Boston University, and the study and paper were both products of a course titled Imagining

Frosty Arctic rose leaves.

Animal Minds, a writing class offered by Professor Holly Schaaf. Now I was even more interested because if the college student Emma Rademacher, majoring in speech, language, and hearing sciences, could pull off such a fine study, so could I, certainly. I wrote to Professor Schaaf and asked if she would pass on my contact information to Emma. Both Holly and Emma responded expressing enthusiasm about my project and wished me luck. I would soon learn I was taking on a bigger challenge than I thought.

Let's check in on the imaginary squirrel. Whenever I travel deep in the trees, particularly near sunset, my eyesight is blemished by indistinct light. I feel a bit out of place, disoriented, harboring notions of insecurity and aloneness.

With a shoulder against a spruce, I watch a squirrel carry a load of cones to a midden at the base of another spruce approximately in the center of its acre-size territory, where it disappears under ground. For a space of several feet encircling the tree's base is a mound of cone scales left by the squirrel (the tree reminiscent of a candle rising from the center of a chocolate cupcake) where it hides its cones in burrows. Sometimes it leaves cones on the surface to eat, tearing them apart and adding to its main cache and home, building the mound of reddish-brown scales, the mound's color a hue like the chickaree's.

That's one of the red squirrel's names, chickaree (only six words removed from chicanery in my edition of *Webster's New Collegiate Dictionary*), and it has lots of names, many derogatory and well-deserved, but here north of Denali, in a wide swath of boreal forest that circles the earth, I've only heard it called red squirrel, or little bastard. A mantra for many people living in the woods is "red is dead." I don't feel that way at all, although I have been annoyed by squirrels. They are only doing what they do, at least that's how I see it, and aside from a ruined special sweater (Doylanne's favorite soft wool outer attire in Alaska's cool autumn) and a well-chewed fabric tool bag, they've done us no harm, yet.

The imaginary squirrel runs back to its targeted tree and tosses more cones to the ground around the base, for indeed, this time in autumn, with freezing temperatures only days away, it's on a mission to survive.

Anchorage-based writer Bill Sherwonit described the end of summer squirrel behavior on the hillside at the edge of Anchorage like this: "Watching squirrels' frenzied movements in backyard spruces, I sensed a life-and-death urgency, as if there were no time to waste." Sherwonit is describing semi-urban squirrels blessed with benevolent human neighbors who supplement larders with bird seed and peanut butter.

Red squirrels everywhere, wilderness as well as in town, rely on cones and nuts (cones in Alaska) to make it through winter, but as omnivores, their diet includes much more than that: insects, grasses, blooms, bulbs, all make the list, as do eggs. Egg-eater is a name that red squirrels have earned. They'll eat most anything it seems, particularly those squirrels that have become familiar with humans. A friend, Jack Evans, while camping near Tolsona, Alaska, watched a red squirrel encounter a pizza box on a picnic table. "We were totally surprised when it dragged an entire slice of pizza up a tree," he said.

This red squirrel tests a cushion on the deck, certainly an interloper.

Reds gnaw on moose antlers when they can, rounding the tips of the tines. Research indicates they may be getting calcium from the antlers. I've tried unsuccessfully to entice squirrels at the homestead with salt, a mineral I figured all animals liked. No luck. Although it is known that squirrels do lick road salt, I've not had wild animals touch salt placed for them to find. Also, no wild animals touched the piles of commercial bird seed I put in the woods near the homestead. I expected these squirrels would ravish the bird seed like the red squirrels do in the backyard at our home, but no, at least not yet. They've stood near the seeds but displayed no interest.

I kept reading about squirrels, and the more I dug, the more I became intrigued. My office writing space (I can't quite call it an office where I trip on grandchildren's toys) turned into a squirrel library. I discovered the book titles and ordered them from the Wasilla library, enough books that the librarians began to look askance at me when I arrived to pick up a new addition. On one occasion the librarian behind the plastic shield (this happened during the COVID years) said, "Wow, this looks like riveting reading." She handed me a slim volume, a 1969 master's thesis titled "Aspects of Red Squirrel (*Tamiasciurus hudsonicus*) Population Ecology in Interior Alaska," by Paul Vincent Krasnowski, on loan from the

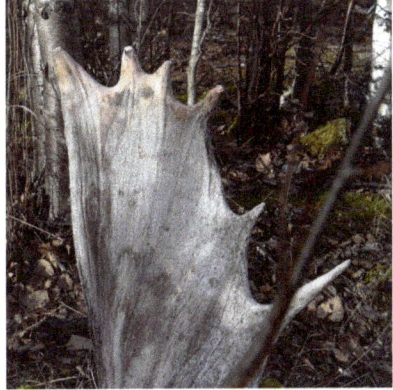

Tines rounded by a gnawing squirrel.

Game Management Library, Alaska Department of Fish and Game. "First time I've seen a book from this library," she said and smiled. I read it that night and liked it. Krasnowski studied squirrel density and distribution around Fairbanks, about one hundred air miles from our homestead. At the end of his study, he included recommendations for future study. One of his suggestions grabbed my attention: "That various methods of collecting red squirrel specimens be evaluated to determine which provide random samples. Sampling of the population must take into account difference between territorial and vagrant squirrels in both population structure and behavior."

Vagrant squirrels, that's what caught my eye. The territorial squirrels are the landowners and masters, and the vagrants are the footloose, wandering squirrels hanging at the edge of middens awaiting their turn. The name, vagrant, sort of works I suppose, but it doesn't quite fit the squirrel hanging at the edge of the midden. I think interloper fits more properly. If the master leaves even for a short time, or is injured, or dies, the unwelcomed squirrel will storm in and take command in a heartbeat. This invasion can happen at any time.

Vagrancy and invasions are stories as old as mankind itself. Some of us may even have our own vagrant or two dwelling at the edge, in the shadows, waiting to invade. On a grander scale, it's the story of epic conflicts (all brutal) like the Roman Conquest or America's western expansion. Someone today, likely a writer of prodigious stature, is writing what will be a great novel about Russia's 2022 invasion of Ukraine. Western Europe is the master and Russia the vagrant.

Russia as a vagrant? I wondered if Vladimir Nabokov wrote about squirrels (he did). I conjectured about squirrels in literature. How are they depicted? The answer is, from what I can tell, like people are portrayed. Since we don't know how animals think or what they think about, we sometimes assume they do so as humans do, which is anthropomorphism, so fiction featuring squirrels as protagonist and antagonist rely on squirrels behaving like humans, which is a huge leap in logic. However, those stories that give squirrels human qualities and go the extra mile to endow them with known behaviors of their species can be special.

Children's books are adorned with adorable squirrels behaving as humans might. *Miss Suzy* by Miriam Young, pictures by Arnold Lobel, 1964, is one of those special books. Miss Suzy, a gray squirrel, lives happily at the top of an oak tree by herself, until the day a gang of red squirrels invades her home and drives her away out into the rain. She finds an abandoned old house and inside a box containing five toy soldiers who are delighted to be set free. I won't spoil the ending because this book is worth finding and reading, but the band of reds are the bad guys, which fits their *modous opporandi*. I will note that red squirrels don't typically band together, being solitary animals, but it's certainly possible. This is a book for small children.

Author M. I. McAllister has written a series of novels featuring a squirrel named Urchin. *The Mistmantle Chronicles*, five books published between 2005 and 2010, geared toward middle grade and older readers, is about anthropomorphic animals with a red squirrel as a main character who performs many heroic deeds over the course of the five books. (For full disclosure, I've only read two of them.) Urchin is a bit different because his coloring is not like a typical red squirrel. The author links animal behavior with actions in the story, not an easy feat, and weaves romance, heroism, and realism into beautifully written tales.

In Beatrice Potter's *The Tale of Squirrel Nutkin*, 1903, we encounter another red squirrel, Nutkin. He has human characteristics and can be easily disliked. He pesters an old owl with riddles to the point that the owl strongly considers putting an end to him, but Nutkin doesn't cross the line to bad squirrel (in my view) and certainly not to dark or sinister squirrel.

*The Adventures of Chatterer the Red Squirrel: The Bedtime*

*Story Books* by Thornton W. Burgess, illustrated by Harrison Cady, 1915, is one of the finest examples of meshing anthropomorphism and animal behavior. Chatterer is one of a long line of animals, along with Reddy Fox, Peter Rabbit, and Ol' Mistah Buzzard, to name a few, that Burgess wrote cleverly and eloquently about during his ninety-one years.

I suppose that's enough of children's books with squirrels as main characters. There are dozens of them, and many have survived the test of time, as they say. A point I want to make is that we hold opinions about squirrels based in part on our reading of children's books and the symbols they reinforce and advance.

What about the heavy hitters in literature, those who were assigned in high school and college? How did they view squirrels?

Low and behold, Vladimir Nabokov, Franz Kafka, Frederick Nietzsche, Anton Chekhov, Herman Melville, F. Scott Fitzgerald, Tobias Wolff, and William James all included squirrels in their writing, according to a *Guardian* article. I looked further for squirrels among some of my favorite authors.

In Ernest Hemingway's story "The Doctor and the Doctor's Wife," logs break away from a log boom and drift to Dr. Adam's land. He hires local Indians to cut the wood up for his use. One of the workers confronts the doctor about his ownership of the logs, making it clear that he doesn't care who owns the logs but pointing out that they don't belong to the doctor. Dr. Adams becomes angry and orders the workers off his land. Dr. Adams and his son go black squirrel hunting. End of story. In Hemingway's abstruse way, we're left with the image of squirrels soon to face the wrath of Dr. Adams and his shotgun.

Red squirrels miraculously appear as if by a magic trick.

In Don Berry's *Trask*, one of the first novels I truly loved, a mountain man seeks enlightenment and discovery in the Oregon coastal mountains. The novel, revered for many reasons—respect of Indian culture and depiction of nature being two of them—is considered one of the most important novels written by an Oregon writer. It also has a fascinating ending. In a euphoric moment *Trask* throws himself headlong and buries his face in the carpet of pine needles, becoming part of the forest floor. The sun warms him and dizzies him with its beauty.

A startled squirrel leaps sideways, then begins to scold Trask who rises to his feet and listens in fascination until he begins to laugh. The more he laughs, the more the squirrel scolds. The laughter pours out of him like a flood.

This is the last page of the novel. The final page! Why did Don Berry use a squirrel in this scene of ecstasy? I believe Berry recognized that the squirrel, a symbolic sentinel throughout the wilderness, is the wild mammal that best illustrates that remote places are where we all will ultimately venture to discover the universe and find ourselves. "Come in," the squirrel calls. "The door is open."

There are lots of other renowned authors who have used squirrels in their writing: Toni Morrison, Mark Twain, William Faulkner, Agatha Christie, Louis L'Amour, and Mary Oliver, to name a few more, and who knows how many writers found a place for one of the most omnipresent, loved, and hated mammals on earth, but here's one more I want to mention. Sarah Orne Jewett's story "The White Heron" is a masterpiece of nature writing. She mentions squirrels two times in her short piece.

Squirrels captured print space in the summer of 2022 when the investigations and hearings on January 6 accelerated, a time when the competition for column inches in major publications must have been fierce. Regardless, squirrels were featured in a story in *The Atlantic* on July 8, 2022. "Admit it, Squirrels are Just Tree Rats: So Why Do We Love One Rodent and Hate the Other," by Jacob Stern, bejeweled their pages—and I loved it. Some people like rats, most don't. Some people hate squirrels, most don't. The two are rodents with many similarities and important differences, and Stern points these out succinctly and humorously, but for me there is no comparison between the two, and that's because I've never seen a rat in the wilderness—aside from a muskrat, which is a rodent close to a beaver, not a squirrel. I view rats as dirty city creatures, whereas squirrels reign in the wilderness or at the fringes of urban parks and grassy knolls on college campuses. Rats are in sewers and dumpsters; squirrels are in trees. (There are, of course, ground squirrels, but we'll leave them alone.) So, there you go, I make Stern's point. Most people like squirrels more than rats. I'm one of them.

I've strayed a bit from the squirrel study, haven't I. Let's head back that way now.

# THREE

# HOW SQUIRRELS MEASURE UP

*Nature speaks in symbols and in signs,*
*And through her pictures human fate divines.*

—John Greenleaf Whittier, "To Charles Sumner"

Emma's study focused on the differences in behaviors among a population of Eastern gray squirrels. She investigated how these urban squirrels responded to humans through habitat selection, boldness, and vigilance. She hypothesized that the squirrels found in the northern areas of the Boston Common Central Burying Ground would be bolder and less vigilant than squirrels found in southern quadrants. Her study supported her hypothesis. She surmised that the northern squirrels were bolder and less vigilant because of habituation to humans (familiarity), density of conspecifics (more of the same species), and efficacy of the canopy cover (the more, the bolder the squirrel).

To test vigilance, she measured flight initiation distance (FID), which was accomplished by measuring the distance between her and the squirrel when it began to run away as she approached slowly. To test boldness, she recorded the time it took for each squirrel to take an almond from her. She did this by sitting in the grass and offering a nut either in her hand or placed beside her. When she gained a squirrel's attention, she started a stopwatch. Emma also recorded qualitative observations about squirrel behavior.

I've never been to the Boston Common Central Burying Ground, but I'm assuming it's similar to city parks and college campuses I've visited. From an aerial photo in Emma's paper, the property resembles a house drawn by a small child with a square and a pointy roof. The roof is called the grassy triangle, and the square is divided into four quadrants—northwest, northeast, southwest, and southeast. The northern quadrants are heavily treed, and the southwest quadrant is the most open. The entire area is bordered by streets and buildings.

It is, of course, quite different than the Alaska wilderness. Our homestead rests under a heavy canopy of birch and white spruce along a small river north of Denali and south of the Yukon River. This year will mark thirty-six consecutive years traveling to one of the most remote and sparsely populated regions in Alaska. I staked the land in the 1980s, built a cabin, and have been going there every year since. Doylanne and I now live there about two months a year. In addition to the cabin, I've built a guest cabin, shed, outdoor shower, a couple outhouses, and a woodshed. We get there by boat, a long, and at times arduous, two-hundred-mile river journey.

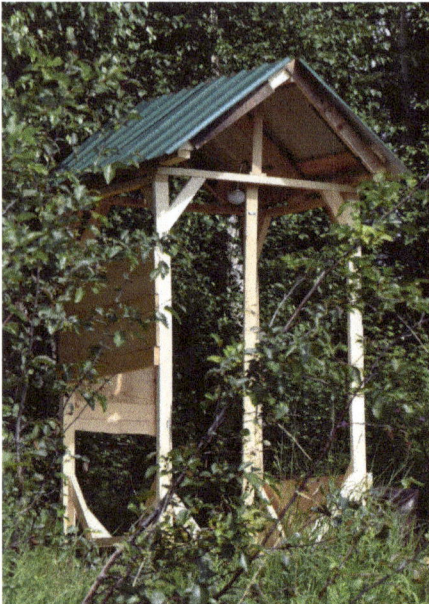

This shower is a new and quite popular addition.

In the spring of 2022, we left our home in Wasilla headed to our homestead to begin the squirrel study. Trees leafed out in their annual explosion along the Parks Highways as we made our way the five hours to the boat launch. Once there, we purchased gasoline—150 gallons at $5.75 a gallon—and were on our way on the river.

The river ran high, so the going was easy, except it took a long time to properly position our load to get the boat on-step. ("On-step" is accelerating a boat to rise above the bow wave, which reduces draw, increases speed, and saves fuel. It's also called planing.) After seven hours dodging sandbars, we camped at a long, white beach, a place we aim for because it's a little more than halfway and has an abundance of driftwood for a camp fire. The beach is also quite large, so we set our camp out in the breeze and away from mosquitoes. A bear would also have to expose itself for a long time to get to us, something they don't like to do.

This black bear looks a little bigger than average.

There's always a bit of concern about bears, which seems to me common sense in a place with more bears than people. And yes, a bear did cross the beach that evening. At first I thought it was a black wolf. I was sitting in a lawn chair near the campfire when the bear stepped out of the trees more than two hundred yards away. Black and gangly, it held still, except for swinging its head in the air. I pointed it out to Doylanne, and she pointed her camera. "No, that's a skinny bear," she said. The bear

A small cabin makes the difference, particularly when rain falls sideways and trees squeal in the wind.

then walked to the river and swam across, soon disappearing in the trees.

We left midmorning and two hours later stopped at the home of friends we've known for more than thirty years, a husband and wife, the only people we've met who live full-time in the region, although I know there are others. He'd been there since the late 1980s and she arrived soon after. They built an extraordinary homestead in the woods. It's amazing that we have known each other for half a lifetime but only talk together about an hour a year. We consider them dear friends. He'd just turned eighty-one and said he was finding it hard to breathe with all the pollen.

Thirty minutes later we were on our way again.

From the boat launch, we navigate four rivers, and we were about to turn onto the fourth, a waterway the color of a red-amber beer in a frosted glass. This is our river, a clear water stream running high. I popped the boat onto step and backed off to the edge of blissful planing for the final hour-long cruise to the cabin.

It had been a magnificent river run, and there we stood at the homestead, it looking just as we'd left it the previous October. I began removing the bear boards from the door when Doylanne said, "Listen, do you hear anything different?" I swatted a few lazy mosquitoes. "I don't hear any squirrels," she said.

I didn't either. At 5:00 pm on May 29, all was silent. "They're here somewhere. Let's get to work and get in this place before the bugs find us," I said.

The squirrel I imagine is standing upside down, attached twenty feet up a spruce, frozen. It's doing that because it's heard something and is at high alert, and because it can. It has a unique anatomical feature allowing it to rotate its hind ankles to grip the wood as if it were climbing upward while facing downward.

Below it is a black bear and two cubs in a lowbush cranberry patch. The large cubs, born the previous spring in a den, begin ascending the spruce. The squirrel changes direction instantly and is in moments at the top of the tree. The mother bear has no intention of following the cubs up the tree, (that would expend far too much energy), but she too, has heard something and has sent the cubs to safety. Its normal day-to-day

On blue days, distance doesn't matter.

*business for squirrels and the bears, a day gathering*
*food and getting fat for the harsh winter about to come.*
*That's what they do.*

At the homestead, black bears tend to show up during early morning, but you can expect to see them any time of day, on every trail, and even where there are no trails. Surprisingly, they aren't as big an animal as some might expect, not here in the interior. I would say, though, that they're big enough to stop a heartbeat and change a mind. I've field-dressed a few and think two hundred pounds is a good, average number for an adult black bear. Some are 250 pounds, and some of the big black bears can be seven feet in height and weight more than three hundred pounds, but the average black bear is the size of a big human. Certainly, black bears grow bigger in other locations. For a comparison, the average adult black bear in New York state weighs 300 pounds where, I suppose, living is just a little easier.

In our region of boreal forest, though, compared to other animals, bears are indeed big; only the moose and the inland grizzly are bigger. Almost all animals here are small. Few approximate the size of a black bear, which is more than 350 times bigger than a squirrel—a significant difference, even greater than the difference between humans and dinosaurs. Humans are closer in size to a T. Rex than a squirrel is to a black bear. An average

Flowers are on display
late May through August.

Blueberries abound in July and August.

Lowbush cranberries ready to be picked
late August and September.

human is two hundred pounds; T. Rex was fifteen thousand pounds—that's seventy-five times bigger. What's my point? There aren't a lot of big animals in the boreal forest of interior Alaska. Only four exceed a hundred pounds: bears, moose, caribou—I've never seen a caribou near our place but know they exist in the foothills of the Alaska Range—and sometimes wolves. That's it.

For humans, bigness is an overrated attribute, I think, unless you play in the NBA or NFL. Big, though, is coveted by many. Tall people make more money over the course of a career—about two dollars more an hour—and 55 percent of women prefer men taller than themselves. Apparently, tall women also find it easier to land modeling jobs. But bigger people also find it harder to climb out of Corvettes, sleep on couches, and climb into small airplanes. So, there are trade-offs. Largess in size for humans is generally desired, but its value is more symbolic than real.

The same is true for wild animals. The advantages of bigness in the wilderness are negligible. There's not much advantage to being large where every day is spent

the occasional black bear, and yes, squirrels. He recently told me he puts peanut butter on his back fence just to watch the squirrels while he drinks his morning coffee. You can take the boy out of the "Bush," but you can't take the "Bush" out of the boy.

An Eastern gray squirrel can weight up to twenty-four ounces, so it can be twice as large as a wee red squirrel. To a little boy, it was indeed a giant, which is a symbol embedded in our psyche from the first stories told to us on our parents' laps. Barry Lopez wrote in *High Country News* magazine in 1998, "human imagination is shaped by the architectures it encounters as a child." The landscape of a parent's lap, the vistas of a remote mine in the Alaska mountains, and the sparkles on a moving stream, all shape who we become.

A black bear cub can climb
a tree in seconds.

As mentioned, regardless of size and species, squirrels have obtained, over thousands of years, a significant symbolic stature. For example, in *Make Prayers to the Raven*, cultural anthropologist Richard K. Nelson points out that a red squirrel historically has a strong spiritual power among Koyukons in interior Alaska, and much of the squirrel's influence was considered negative. For example, if a "man wounds one of these animals and it escapes, it is a sign that his wife is unfaithful—and its spirit will cause her to die." Also at night, the ordinary names of the red squirrel were not to be spoken, or bad things would happen. As well, it was bad luck to even hear a chattering squirrel at night.

There are positive interpretations as well. A common theme by Native American writers is the need for connection with the land. David Moore, English professor and scholar of Native American Studies, described making a connection with nature through a squirrel on *Reflections West* on Montana Public Radio:

> Then the other morning, here in Missoula, I had a conversation with a talkative pine squirrel. Smaller than the invasive Eastern gray squirrels imported by my settler culture, the pine squirrel is beautiful with its gray-green back and cream-colored chest and belly. It sat right outside our open bedroom window, awaking me early, and chattering, "Wake up! Pay attention!"

Moore references N. Scott Momaday's book *The Way to Rainy Mountain* (1969). Momaday had this to say about connections:

> East of my grandmother's house the sun rises out of the plain. Once in his life a man ought to concentrate his mind upon the remembered earth, I believe. He ought to give himself up to a particular landscape in his experience, to look at it from as many angles as he can, to wonder about it, to dwell upon it. He ought to imagine that he touches it with his hands at every season and listens to the sounds that are made upon it. He ought to imagine the creatures there and all the faintest motions of the wind. He ought to recollect the glare of noon and all the colors of the dawn and dusk.

The theme of healing through relationships with land and animals is prevalent throughout the genre of nature writing. A beautifully written example is *Raising Ourselves*, by Alaska author Velma Wallis, a Gwitch'in Athabaskan. She credits living on the land as her ancestors once did—hunting, trapping, and fishing—for giving her hope and confidence and providing a way beyond the dysfunction of her upbringing.

That evening, just after going to bed, we heard gnawing on our guest cabin.

# FOUR

# SQUIRRELS, KNIGHTS, AND COWBOYS

*It was like a friendship between morning and
evening—all freshness and sunshine on one side,
and all gentleness and peace on the other.*

—Harriet Beecher Stowe, "Uncle Lot"

My squirrel study would have three parts: qualitative observations, a test for vigilance, and a test for boldness. I was ready and had my pocket-sized booklet for field notes handy, but the squirrels stayed hidden. I hiked back into the woods and did occasionally hear chattering but never saw one. Doylanne watched for squirrels too.

The river ran high, not dropping as we expected. So I imagined that Denali melted, the beginning of one of the greatest ecological disasters in world history happening before our very eyes, a barren, jagged peak rising above the ruins in a dystopian world, and why wouldn't I think that? There weren't any squirrels, and there should have been, not until June 2 when Doylanne spotted the first North American red squirrel at our homestead.

We'd finished morning coffee with the door of the cabin open to a brilliant day, the screen densely dotted with mosquitoes attempting entry, when Doylanne saw it at the bottom of the deck steps. I shuffled softly toward the squirrel, and it darted away. I measured the distance between where I stood and from where the squirrel departed: eleven feet, eight inches. I followed the squirrel to the woodshed.

The squirrel and I froze for a few moments. When I moved, it sprinted off, its first steps toward me, then veered into the woods. I measured: thirteen feet, five inches. I now had two entries. My study was underway.

A scorcher day lay ahead, the morning temperature already nearly seventy degrees. We went about our chores and projects while watching for squirrels but didn't see any. We didn't talk, usual behavior for us when we're working closely but with different tasks and deep in our own thoughts. That evening we sat on the deck until midnight when the twilight gently dissolved to a brief darkness.

The clear river still hadn't receded. Ordinarily, high water is always dirty water, but not now. Denali might actually be melting. The ice below the active layer of soil certainly was.

Melting permafrost is a grave concern for us, and our actions have contributed to damaged land. All the logs for the cabin were felled and pulled with a chainsaw winch to the building site, resulting in sunken spots and sink holes that fill with water. Simply walking on the ground can create indentions and enough wear to melt the ice eighteen inches below. There's ample evidence of this occurring across our property. We all live on a warming earth.

The squirrel I imagine is a recluse, which is typical for red squirrels. It's territorial and parsimonious and not sociable with other squirrels, not communal as some species, particularly as ground squirrels, are prone to be. When one is seen chasing another down the length of a log or across the yard, a fight is likely underway, or the mating game has ensued. Squirrels defend their food caches, chasing away vagrants (aka potential intruders) and the female squirrel allows males to chase her until she's ready to mate, and then it believed, she chooses the one that most impressed her during the race. She will often mate with more than one so the second or third might eventually get his chance. But this isn't the season for mating. This is spring.

While thinking about how squirrels select their mates, it dawned on me why squirrels were absent from our yard. The month of May, perhaps the most beautiful month in the north, is when many animals are having babies and protecting nests. In the wild, spring is mostly about birth, and here the birthing was done. Now the tiny creatures delicately breathed along a perilous journey to survive the first weeks of most vulnerability. The same is true in Boston Buried Grounds or at Harvard Square, I suppose, but in the Alaska wilderness there are simply more predators. There are also no free meals, no seeds or peanut butter, seldom any people to scare away the adventuresome wild cat.

That's not to say that urban squirrels aren't wild. My experience walking through city parks, often encountering squirrels, has convinced me they obviously aren't domesticated, but they have resources not available to wilderness squirrels, and it appears their lives are not multiple-alarm fires like their cousins in the wild. The wilderness is simply different.

Our place in the wilds feels mislaid and unknown, at times, a lost place where there is no reason for practical people to go. A federal wildlife officer I know who's been across Alaska working for years, calls our region a no man's land. Why would anyone go there, a place certainly wild, yet surprisingly so unproductive: no gold, no riches, no silver salmon, no people.

I studied the word *wild* a bit and soon found myself in the Middle Ages when the word *wilde* was first used in writing. I was soon magically transported back to high school English class (back to the early 1970s) and Mr. Smith (not his real name), who apparently thought all of us in our small logging town on the Oregon coast were born under a rock and destined to stay lodged there, and his remedy was to require us to memorize passages from Middle English. Classical literature, even a spoonful, would make us all more urbane and worldly, and ultimately, save us, from what, none of us knew, but he must have known because he told us every day we needed to somehow escape from the ill-conceived human experiment of which we were subjects. I suspect he tried to motivate us to learn something and didn't really feel that way because the place was in fact beautiful, and I would learn over the years that we attended a pretty good little school. One passage was the first sentence of Chaucer's Prologue to *The Canterbury Tales*. It was a despised assignment, generally, but for some reason I did it, and frankly, ended up enjoying the challenge. Before this assignment, the longest thing I'd ever memorized was a telephone number and a jelly sandwich recipe.

Whan that Aprille with his shoures soote,
The droghte of March hath perced to the roote,
And bathed every veyne in swich licóur
Of which vertú engendred is the flour;

Whan Zephirus eek with his swete breeth
Inspired hath in every holt and heeth
The tendre croppes, and the yonge sonne
Hath in the Ram his halfe cours y-ronne,
And smale foweles maken melodye,
That slepen al the nyght with open ye,
So priketh hem Natúre in hir corages,
Thanne longen folk to goon on pilgrimages,
And palmeres for to seken straunge strondes,
To ferne halwes, kowthe in sondry londes;
And specially, from every shires ende
Of Engelond, to Caunterbury they wende,
The hooly blisful martir for to seke,
That hem hath holpen whan that they were seeke.

My former classmates who might read this are likely winching. I was inspired. I attended college and majored in English where I read, because they were required reading in my degree program, many of the twenty-four Canterbury tales.

One of them, more than all the others, I found most fun to read: there once was this knight unlike all the others. He didn't rescue damsels in distress or slay mighty dragons. His named was Sir Thopas and he meandered through the countryside searching for the Elf Queen whom he wanted to marry because the ladies in town weren't quite pretty enough for him. Along the way he tracks and hunts the wilde beast, the hare. The tale is satire and the rhythm and rhyme purposely not up to Chaucer's par, so much so that an innkeeper eventually begs him to stop telling the wretched story. From the tale:

And so it fell upon a day,
For sooth as I you telle may,
Sir Thopas would out ride;
He worth upon his steede gray,
And in his hand a launcegay,
A long sword by his side.
He pricked through a fair forest,
Wherein is many a wilde beast,
Yea, bothe buck and hare;

Chaucer uses wilde as an adjective, uncultivated, untamed, undomesticated, uncontrolled, but it can be used as a noun, verb, and adverb as well. It means beyond, out there in place and manner.

Where homo sapiens are outnumbered by everything.

Jumping to Chaucer's tale about Sir Thopas, written in 1387, may seem a stretch in this book, but the knight relegated to a mighty hunter of the big bunny rabbit is a theme relevant to this story, I think. Sir Thopas is a buffoon in literature, scoffed at by all the true lovers of knighthood, even Chaucer, the author. The feats of knights abound in history and mythology, but Chaucer picked a bit at poor Sir Thopas, the knight on a mission-drift across the English countryside.

The medieval knight is much like another imaginary, mythical character: the American cowboy. There once were real cowboys (and there are still some), but the image of the cowboy we are most familiar with was created in stories, as was the knight, of course. The two share a similar mythology: the male loner with great skills and courage, bigger than life, crosses the hinterlands in search of self and independence, separated from the civilized world by space and deeds, who embraces the core principles of chivalry, unshackled from the grip of humankind. He also is usually a large man, though there are exceptions. Knights and cowboys are clearly larger than life.

But alas, knights and cowboys, as we've come to know them, reside in story books.

It's fascinating, and sad, that in the wilderness, the big ones, the king, queens, knights and cowboys of the wilds, those dominant animals, those that usually rule the moment, are the first to perish as their conditions change, particularly when the changes involved homo sapiens. Yuval Noah Harari in *Sapiens: A Brief History of Humankind* points out that the expansion and dominance of *Sapiens* led to "one of the biggest and swiftest ecological disasters to befall the animal kingdom," with the hardest hit the "large furry animals," which makes sense, because there's obviously more meat on a big animal than a small one. Harari writes that about half of the world's big animals were hunted to extinction before the invention of the wheel.

The small red squirrel, although struggling in many parts of the world because of the invasive stern gray squirrel, is doing OK, particularly well in the Alaska wilderness.

On June 12 I encountered my third squirrel. I had stored spruce kindling in a cardboard box, all pieces of one-by-twos and two-by-fours, the extra fragments, leftovers from a building project. I'd placed the box on top of a stack of birch quarter rounds in the woodshed, divided between a spruce side and a birch side. Anyway, the squirrel was vigorously tearing at the cardboard. I watched it run off with a couple loads before I tested for vigilance. Following the procedure used by Emma, I stepped slowly toward the squirrel after I knew it was aware of my presence. Eight feet, that's how close I was to it before it sprang away with a mouthful of cardboard.

Wild animals love these breaks in the forest. An animal will soon reveal itself.

I was surprised when it returned while I measured the distance. It didn't stay, but it rapidly ran by me, up the wood pile and away, disappearing in the brush.

I suspect it was taking my measure. To apply some anthropomorphism, maybe it was asking, "What is that strange creature. What are its thoughts? Why does it exist? What good is it?" It might have been philosophizing about me, as I must admit, I was about it. Squirrels are well suited as a subject for philosophical inquiry.

Red squirrels in a hot spot, such as when a predator is near, are known to hug a spruce while attempting to blend with the bark. They also circle trees to avoid predators and gnarly tree limbs, and always, as they perform these maneuvers, their backs are exposed, and their bellies are hidden against the tree. American philosopher William James, a scholar considered one of the leading thinkers of the nineteenth and twentieth centuries, thought about squirrels and knew their behavior. He most certainly watched them scurry about Harvard Yard and while on camping sojourns with his rowdy friends. James used a squirrel in one of his most noted philosophical questions to clarify the philosophy of pragmatism. It goes like this:

> Some years ago, being with a camping party in the mountains, I returned from a solitary ramble to find everyone engaged in a ferocious metaphysical dispute. The corpus of the dispute was a squirrel—a live squirrel supposed to be clinging to one side of a tree trunk; while over against the tree's opposite side, a human being was imagined to stand. This human witness tries to get sight of the squirrel by moving rapidly round the tree, but no matter how fast he goes, the squirrel moves as fast in the opposite direction and always keeps the tree between himself and the man so that never a glimpse of him is caught. The resultant metaphysical problem now is this: DOES THE MAN GO AROUND THE SQUIRREL OR NOT? He goes around the tree, sure enough, and the squirrel is on the tree; but does he go around the squirrel?

It's interesting that James's friends were engaged in a "metaphysical dispute"; rather than what bait to use in the lake teeming with brook trout, but maybe James just missed that discussion. Half of the camping party thought the man obviously circled the squirrel and the other half concluded that it wasn't possible because the man never came between the squirrel and the tree. So, it fell on James to break the tie. He explained around the campfire after a thoughtful analysis and, I'm just guessing here, a stiff drink or two that both sides were right—and wrong; therefore, it didn't matter. Since there was no consequence, they were arguing about nothing, not at all a pragmatic thing to do. James began the second chapter of his book *Pragmatism* with the above scenario, and the question: what good is it, if it isn't useful? He also reinforced his message subliminally by using a squirrel.

Certainly, others embraced pragmatism as well: Charles Sanders Peirce, philosopher and the father of pragmatism; John Dewey, philosopher and education reformer; and my mother-in-law are three notable ones. The first two I've read about and the third I knew well.

I don't know if Bernita, a truly lovely person, was aware of the philosophy of pragmatism, but I do know it's what she practiced. She's notable to me because she influenced Doylanne and is one of the reasons we can't throw anything away because, as all pragmatists know, one day, if we live long enough, it might prove useful.

Our son Jed, on his fifth birthday, represented this philosophy in a way that might have made William James proud: Doylanne and his three brothers gathered around him as he faced his birthday cake with five flickering candles. I stood back a few feet with a camcorder. Placed among the burning candles were small plastic toys recently extracted from the toy box. We waited for Jed to blow out the candles. He positioned himself to gain the best advantage to vanquish the flames with one mighty puff. He looked to Doylanne and she encouraged him. As he was about to commence, one of the plastic toys caught on fire, the flame advancing beyond those of the candles. We all burst into laughter, all of us except Jed. He stared in disbelief and then began to cry, then to sob. He then blurted out a clause that will always be a part of him within our family, a slice of every birthday he has: "That could have been useful." Jed was an adherent of pragmatism.

So are squirrels, and I believe William James knew that well and is why he included one to frame his famous philosophical question. Squirrels are always planning, building, moving, and keeping their backs to the predators circling it around the tree (I fit on that side of the argument), always posturing for survival. They are useful too. These tiny animals are an important link in the northern wilderness food chain.

# FIVE

# SQUIRRELS ARE EDIBLE

*Getting what we know to dawn on us is a*
*fundamental human bugaboo.*

—William Least Heat-Moon, *River Horse*

In the wilderness, there aren't many squirrel-human encounters. Squirrels are abundant, people aren't. Red squirrels stay close to home, occupying about one acre their entire lives. If home isn't along a river or a well traveled snowmachine trail, they have no opportunity to see a human, so in that way they are quite lucky. As already alluded to and on which history has been clear, *Homo sapiens*—large mammals with insatiable appetites—are the deadliest of all animals.

Years ago, a man (I won't use his name because this short story might embarrass some in his family) attended a wedding reception held in a park on the Oregon coast. The bride's family was there, the groom's family too. In fact, the man was the groom's dad. The man didn't feel welcome, though, because he had long been outside his family. He'd left them years before to do more fun things than work and raise a family. Sometimes, though, he'd show up for weeks at a time and hang around at the edges. He hadn't received an invitation to this party and wasn't too happy about being ignored.

As the children played and the adults talked, squirrels dashed around their picnic tables, eating the morsels dropped to the green

Grizzlies are rare in our area, but they do show up from time to time.
This one joined us one day for breakfast.

grass. Western gray squirrels scurried about and were decent-sized, the man thought, though not as big as the squirrels he had hunted while growing up along the Wabash River. There he'd killed and eaten lots of fox squirrels, a big tree squirrel.

The man went to his car and from the trunk pulled out a .22 caliber rifle, a lever action beauty he'd used many times on small game. The party attendees froze when he walked slowly toward them, his eyes focused up a Douglas fir. He stopped a few yards away from the tables and aimed the rifle into the tree. Pop! A Western gray fell to the grass. The man picked up the squirrel. "I'll eat this tonight," he said. He left then, pulling away into the quivering haze of a hot summer day.

I know, not a very pleasant story, but it illustrates a central theme in this book. The man didn't kill the squirrel because he was hungry that afternoon, not at all. He did it because he could, and by doing so then, in the manner he chose, he became a frightening figure to those at the party, and in his eyes, a bigger, more commanding force. The man felt unwelcomed, and I suspect, unworthy, that day at the picnic, but by shooting the squirrel, he felt larger, capable, and more powerful, and by walking away into the haze with his kill, he left an indelible impression—the Shane cowboy moment all western movie watchers know so well, which is what he hoped to accomplish. Those who perceive themselves larger and more powerful must always feel that way in order to be content. They do this often by living a story for all to see. It's the old west novel played out in real time and in person: good versus bad, urban versus rural, wilderness versus civilization, educated versus uneducated, rich versus poor, and on and on, and as James Plath wrote in his essay, "Shadow Rider: The Hemingway Hero as Western Archetype," it's all wrapped in an "uncomplicated plot that revolves around the moral character of the hero."

He probably ate the squirrel. He'd certainly eaten lots of them, and he wasn't alone. Squirrels have always been hunted by humans. Squirrels are food, and humans, three hundred and fifty times bigger, are quite clever at dispatching them.

I know a family that has at times relied on North American red squirrels as food. Not too far from our place in the woods, about two hours away by river, a couple, dear friends, live full-time. They've lived there for decades. Sitting back off the river a couple hundred feet is one of the most beautiful log homes I've ever seen. They built it after living for years in a tiny, partially underground cabin while they trapped and lived off the land. He was a master trapper and she a master gardener. It worked for them in that small place—the size of a bedroom in a typical American home—but eventually they upgraded to a beautiful log home they constructed by hand. They lived in a stronghold of North American red squirrels, and these squirrels often got into things they shouldn't have, so our friends were on alert for them to protect their property. They also were hungry at times, particularly in the spring when the vegetables had diminished to rationing portions, and the moose was all consumed. During those times, squirrels became an important source of food. "We've hunted squirrels for meat many times. That's all we had," one of them told us.

Other mammals hunt squirrels too: lynx, wolves, coyotes, weasels, mink, marten, black bears, grizzlies, and foxes, as do the avian animals: great horned, great gray, and short-eared owls; bald and golden eagles; northern goshawks, sharp-shinned hawks, peregrine falcons, and ravens.

So the going is always tough for the red squirrel, and it never relents. I've killed a few myself, as have my sons, all starting with a BB-gun. Jack, our oldest son, tells this story: "I shot a squirrel near the shed when we lived out on Pittman Road and took off running with it down the hill to the house to show Mom. When I got to the bottom of the hill, the squirrel came back to life. There were a few intense seconds before I finished it off with a rock." That's a story that Doylanne somehow suppressed. I asked her if she remembered Jack and the squirrel, and she didn't.

Another son, Jed, attended Columbia University in Manhattan. He caused quite a stir when he hung up a dry squirrel hide in his John Jay dormitory room. Students stopped by and looked, astonished that someone would do something so cruel as to kill a

Mom and her twins. The river is perhaps the safest place for them.

squirrel. Jed told them it was okay and certainly ethical because he ate it. After he graduated, he brought the squirrel hide with him back to Alaska.

Wild squirrels live short lives. My imaginary squirrel is lucky. It survived its first brutal winter. Its chances now for survival, as it is more than a year old and fully grown, are good, but even so, it only has a life expectancy of about five years, though it is believed that some live ten years. Adult red squirrels, lightning fast, can hide in a rose's shadow and hug a spruce and blend with the bark. They are difficult to see from above as well as below. Michael Steele, in *North American Tree Squirrels*, writes that the tree squirrel benefits from a phenomenon called countershading:

A light-colored underside is covered by a relatively dark upper side. Advantages accrue in several ways with this type of coloration. When a squirrel forages on the ground, the darkened, grizzled dorsal pelage effectively camouflages the squirrel from predators above. When foraging in trees, a squirrel is camouflaged from below because of the pale underside set against the light-colored sky, whereas, darkened from above by the shadow of the body, the underside does not stand out to cue an aerial predator as to the squirrel's location.

I'm sure I missed lots of them as they hugged spruce trees, but I was accustomed to them just being there, making their presence known by zipping by and scolding me, and that just wasn't happening at the homestead. For some reason that spring, it wasn't a very pragmatic thing for a squirrel to do.

My study floundered. I heard squirrels in the trees, but they stayed hidden. I walked north from the cabin a quarter mile upstream and encountered none. I went down river for nearly a mile, and although squirrels were near me, (I heard the chattering) they weren't showing themselves.

At my outhouse, upstream from the cabin, one moaned every morning when I arrived. The sound came from up in a tree, but I never caught a glimpse. On one day in March 2019, Emma encountered eight squirrels at the Boston Common Central Burying Ground. In a month at the homestead, late May through June—three for me.

I also faced a challenge with the boldness test in the study. As you recall, this was the test where Emma sat with a nut either in her hand or near her and timed how long it took for a squirrel to come and take it from her. There are no nuts in the trees at our homestead, only cones. So I used those. I set out small piles of cones on stumps across the property and watched. I began noticing scales on and near the stumps the third week of our trip, but I never saw a squirrel at the piles.

We left the homestead to head back to town at the end of June disappointed with the deflated study but intent on getting back at it in September.

# PART II

The forest crowds the river and hides the animals.

# SIX

# SCHOOL MASCOTS

*If you have built castles in the air, your work*
*need not be lost; that is where they should*
*be. Now put the foundations under them.*

—Henry David Thoreau, *Walden*

After returning home that spring, I worked on building a garden shed and repairing an outboard motor; the first task I accomplished. With August and its changing colors came high school football, and I followed the start of the Alaska high school football season, not so much by sitting in the stands as by reading reports in the paper and on the Internet. Games begin in mid-August with the final games contested in mid-October. I wondered about athletes becoming the images they create and the mythologies we create for them—young athletes wearing jerseys adorned with Moose, Warriors, Knights, Hawks, Cougars, Bears, and Eagles, to name a few, who often play in snow-filled skies and freezing temperatures in Alaska, exemplifying the fierceness and power of their mascots. That got me thinking again about squirrels.

I called Mary Kate Johnston, former principal of Swanson Elementary School in Palmer, Alaska, a school with a squirrel as its mascot, and asked how students, parents, and staff like their mascot. She had this to say: "What a mighty mascot, huh? I always thought it was the perfect mascot for a school of four through eight-year-olds: little, impulsive, fast-moving critters. We had a sign at the school entrance with a large tree squirrel and a sign under it that read, 'Planting the Seeds of Learning' because the kids were just starting out on their schooling journey. The parent, kids, and staff love the mascot."

I went poking around more and found that Swanson Elementary is not alone. There's Central Cass High School in Casselton, North Dakota, the Home of the Squirrels; and Azusa Pacific University in Azusa, California, that changed its mascot from the Cougars to the Squirrels in 2020. *The Washington Post* ran a story in 2014 on this topic. Here's what writer John Kelly found: at Mary Julia Baldwin College in Staunton, Virginia, Gladys the Fighting Squirrel is the mascot; an albino squirrel is the mascot of Oberlin College; a black squirrel is the mascot for Haverford College in Pennsylvania; a gray squirrel is the mascot at the University of Stirling in Scotland (Kelly points out that a gray squirrel is an invasive species in the UK); and to end this list celebrating the squirrels' influence in education, Chipmunks rule at Archbishop Chapelle High School in Metairie, Louisiana. I suspect there are dozens more like these across America and the world. In case you're wondering what the most popular high school mascots in America are (be assured squirrels missed the list), here's what MaxPreps, a website that covers high school sports nationally, reports the top ten are: counting down, 10. Knights, 9. Cougars, 8. Lions, 7. Indians, 6. Warriors, 5. Wildcats, 4. Panthers, 3. Bulldogs, 2. Tigers, and number one, Eagles. That's interesting and relevant to this discussion because as we know, eagles eat squirrels. By the way, Doylanne and I attended high school in a small Oregon coast logging town that named the Boomer, a mountain beaver, its mascot. On the rodent family tree, it's closest to the squirrel. So, like squirrels, mountain beavers aren't particularly high on the animal pecking order and are difficult to make look very tough on jerseys whenever there's a desire to do that. But looks aren't everything. I must insert here for all the Boomers who have gone, and those still headed to the hallowed halls of Toledo High School, we are pretty darn tough rodents, noted for strong forearms, according to scientists.

*A bald eagle landed near the top of a spruce only a few trees away from my imagined squirrel. The chickaree froze in its safe place shielded within dense spruce* evergreen branches and began clicking and chucking, a vigorous chattering phrase meant to alert the predator, not other squirrels in the vicinity as would seem the proper thing to do. Red squirrels are asocial and don't care much about what happens to their conspecifics. In this instance, the squirrel notified the eagle: "I'm here; you're there; I just want you to know."

The bald eagle prefers fish but will eat most anything.

The bald eagle's nest rested on a long limb extending from a massive old spruce two corners upriver. Its partner and an already large offspring hatched that spring peered over the edge of the five-foot-wide nest, watching the river and waiting for the eagle to return with a meal. Eagles eat mostly fish, but an animal crossing an opening is easy prey. The squirrel stayed safe within the branches of the spruce. Eagles, large and majestic, have an uncanny ability to sit still and wait for creatures to forget they've arrived, and that's what this eagle was doing. What was at first easy to see because of its dark feathers and contrasting white head and tail, which took five years to attain, became an inconspicuous part of the wilderness room, which is the power of stillness and silence. The squirrel forgot about the eagle and began moving again in the tree. The eagle dropped to an opening and snatched a rabbit that made its fatal mistake by dashing into the open. The squirrel froze again and watched the carnage transpire in the small meadow near its spruce.

Bloodshed and wilderness are companions. What lives in the wild eats something else that lives there. There is no other way. That's a difficult reality for many of us. I cringe watching nature documentaries showing lions running down antelope, but I know it occurs and, in fact, must happen in order for lions to survive. Here in the boreal forest, wolves pursue moose, lynx pounce on rabbits, and marten chase squirrels around tree trunks. The hunt never ends. Animals have their preferred meals (for instance, as already mentioned, eagles prefer fish), but most have other acceptable fare, and for many in the boreal forest, the abundant squirrel is on the list.

The eagle lifted off with the rabbit and rapidly disappeared beyond the tree crowns, and the squirrel gnawed on a cone with its four incisors, two on top and two on bottom, the scales dropping softly to the earth. The squirrel chewed the seeds with its molars and swallowed its meal while seated on a swaying branch with a royal view of the ever-changing north face of North America's highest mountain. The wind howled at the peak, and an orographic cloud balanced near, a massive structure resembling a lens and aptly named *Altocumulus lenticularis*, a work of unfathomable natural art that would disappear as rapidly as it formed.

A brave, diminutive animal witnessed it all, very much in control.

# SEVEN

# SQUIRREL STUDY IN ACTION

*Certainty is for those who have learned
and believed only one truth.*

—Richard Nelson, *Make Prayers to the Raven*

I bought a new outboard in the summer of 2022. I was lucky to find one available, or some might say, unlucky. The supply-chain mess turned outboard engines into gold.

I broke-in the new engine on August 31, our first day on the river, a day when clouds resembled slices of purple potatoes frying in a skillet. I kept the RPMs at 3,000 for the first couple of hours, making the early miles of the journey a slugfest into a gray world. We camped on the river near dark, surprised we hadn't seen more boats with September 1, the first day of moose hunting season, just hours away.

We ran a hundred miles upstream the next day, most of it at 4,000 RPM, not sufficient to push the heavy load on-step. The weather improved with each hour, and we camped in sunshine with a view of Denali. I had no intention of shooting a moose, even if one walked right up and said hello. I'd loaded my rifle but only for protection, in case a pack of wolves raided our boat (would never happen), or a bear jumped into the bow and tried to break into the cabin (could happen, but highly unlikely), or a squirrel tried to run off with one of Doylanne's sweaters (the most probable, but still highly unlikely). I loaded my rifle because we were traveling in the Alaska wilderness, and it seemed the practical thing to do.

On the third day, we arrived at the homestead. Yellow and russet birch leaves fluttered, the small river sparkled like a morning frost, and shadows of the tall spruce marked pathways across the cleared portion of the property and into the woods, as if they welcomed us home. A squirrel dashed from the woodshed.

I was ready for stage two of my squirrel study. Fifty feet north, behind our guest cabin, not far beyond the cleared edge, rests a central midden, an active structure I first discovered decades ago. A midden is a castle consisting of many holes and tunnels. This large midden would have been home to many dominant squirrels through the years. I measured the distance from the river to the midden—one hundred and ten feet. That made sense. Research has shown that these large middens are generally in the middle of an acre. An acre is 208 by 208 feet, so the squirrel would range roughly a hundred feet in each direction from the midden. This squirrel, the one now at the helm, often ran through our yard.

Hiding under the cabin, munching on a cone.

Right away I noticed three different squirrels in our vicinity. One lived in the central midden (I'll call him the "main" squirrel); another, much smaller and likely an adolescent, lived beneath a spruce visible from the back window (west side); and the third, an adult, often ventured from up river, farther west to the edge of the clearing, perhaps to a line that delineated its boundary with the squirrel that claimed the area that encompassed our cabin. I frequently encountered this squirrel when I meandered down the curvy trail to my outhouse.

The little squirrel looked half the size of the other two. The first time I saw it, I didn't recognize what it was. I watched out the back window while thumbing through Jules Verne's *The Fur Company* when I noticed a ball on the ground. Spherical shapes are not common in the boreal forest. My first thought was fungi of some sort, maybe a puffball, but those I'd seen were white. With its tail curled over its back, the squirrel was round, looked like an apple (that couldn't be, though, not here) and would easily fit in my palm. The apple soon defied gravity and tore up the nearest tree. This squirrel would be my first study entry.

A small but important building at the homestead. An outhouse usually gets built right away.

Here's how that adventure went: On September 8, just after noon, the temperature 45 degrees with overcast skies, the tiny squirrel dashed across the trail between the cabin and the woodshed. My arms were full of wood for the stove, so I delivered those to the wood box and grabbed a tape measure. The squirrel stopped on a stump in the back yard and chewed on a spruce cone. It paused when it saw me but immediately went back to eating. I stepped slowly and as softly a I could but didn't get close. It sprung away at twenty-two feet, ten inches, disappearing up the spruce a few feet from the stump.

I saw it again the next day at the base of the tree it had ascended the day before. The air warm for fall, like a can of evaporated milk left too close to the woodstove, the sky blue and crowded with fluffy cumulus clouds. The squirrel circled the tree several times then came to a rest on the ground and began gnawing on a cone. I watched this squirrel all day. It ran up the tree and jumped between branches, always returning to the base of the spruce tree. I imagined it growing to full-size, another few ounces at most, and perhaps one day occupying the main midden. It ran away at nine feet. I never saw that little squirrel after that day.

On September 11, 7:05 pm, Doylanne spotted a squirrel on the bottom step of the river side of the cabin. She alerted me and I crept toward it. The squirrel was surrounded by scales, indicating it had been there for some time. It held its ground until I was four feet, three inches away. It ran into the tall grass at the river's edge. I think it was the squirrel from the west intruding much too far into another's territory. Perhaps it grew accustomed to my presence because of my trips upriver to the outhouse, or maybe it just knew I was too slow to catch it or knew it was the subject of a study and too valuable to harm.

The next day, the 12th, at 4:15 pm, near the central midden north of the cabin, the main squirrel and I faced off for several minutes before I began my advance. It bolted at nine feet, four inches. This squirrel, the monarch of the midden behind the guest cabin, was also likely becoming familiar with Doylanne and me.

I hate loud bangs in the wilderness forest, like those reverberating, ear-busting sometime-sounds of dropped metal roofing panels, but I created those sounds one afternoon while rearranging a few panels of metal roofing behind the shed. The sounds didn't seem to bother the main squirrel watching me. With a gigantic mushroom in its mouth, it sat on the bottom branch of a spruce, about eye height to me, frozen. I approached the squirrel, slowly, until it dashed away at ten feet, scampering to the ground and over the midden to another nearby spruce, springing to a branch and disappearing in the evergreen. I thought about that squirrel's escape route. Why didn't it simply run into a hole in the midden?

●

Certainty doesn't exist—anywhere. I suppose that is a terrifying thought to some, as it is to me at times. What could be certain? Not the prospect of rain, nor the promise of sun, not the hordes of mosquitoes, nor armies of advancing ants. Or, and I find this most disconcerting, that morning will come. That's why the squirrel led its predator, me, beyond the midden to another tree, just as a duck plays its wounded wing trick on the river, leading threats beyond the nest and its loved ones. It can never be sure.

A red squirrel's life is the final movie scene. The thriller ending, the chase that ends it all. But for a squirrel this scene is first played in the beginning and loops and loops. Squirrels live tragic lives that we abhor contemplating, existences with brief moments of bliss and serenity most certainly to be interrupted by mayhem.

On September 20, Doylanne alerted me to gnawing in the woodshed, so I set forth to capture another study entry. The main squirrel saw me coming but didn't react. It stopped chewing once but didn't move. I stepped closer and closer until I could clearly see its whiskers sticking horizontally from its cheeks, straight, guitar strings stretched along an invisible neck, humming in the fall breeze. I slowly extended an empty hand, palm up, wondering. It then darted, disappearing like a last breath.

It dawned on me then, that moment, when I marveled at how close I came to that wild animal, that I might be contributing to this wild squirrel's early demise. This squirrel would not encounter another large animal like me, not one satisfied with inching closer for a good look.

On September 21, at 10:00 am, I came within six feet of the same squirrel in the same spot. My study entries were adding up.

Later that day, in the evening when the first hints of twilight settled on the land, upriver a quarter mile where I made boards from a wind-blown spruce with a chainsaw mill, a new squirrel became an

This squirrel gradually became more comfortable with me nearby.

entry. This one wasn't having much of it. It sprinted away at twenty feet. Shortly after, I hiked off the river beyond a sink hole, fifty feet at least, and found a midden, probably the one belonging to this squirrel. But I couldn't be certain.

Cumulus clouds usually mean a nice warm day lies ahead,
but these are heavily weighted with water. So, no bets.

# EIGHT

# ANIMALS IN SQUIRELLAND

*Wilderness without wildlife is just scenery.*

—Lois Crisler

Our imaginary squirrel is a main squirrel. Its domain is secure and well protected for the moment, and that splinter of time is enough. But because squirrels don't concern themselves with the future—i.e., there's no such thing as a neurotic, paranoid squirrel—it's unlikely they care. They live in now. Our squirrel makes a death-defying leap to an adjoining spruce without a second thought. The branch it lands upon bends but doesn't break, and the squirrel maneuvers down the spruce to the ground where it encounters a frog. The squirrel, an omnivore, bounds for the wood frog but is a fraction slow, and the frog disappears in a black pool of melted ice. For a red squirrel, it's bounce, duck, jab, retreat, attack—that's its life.

Frogs here are called wood frogs—peculiar, beautiful animals that freeze during the winter and thaw in the spring. At some point in the fall, they burrow into the mud and slowly turn to ice cubes—it's thought that about two-thirds of the frog freezes—and then miraculously they become nimble again in the spring.

The river provides relief from bugs and protection from predators.

From Bill Sherwonit's *Animal Stories:*

"Just as remarkable as their winter freeze-up is the wood frogs' springtime meltdown. The frogs thaw from inside out. First the heart begins to beat (though scientists don't know exactly how it's 'jump-started'), then the brain and other organs kick into gear, and glucose levels return to normal."

Our squirrel doesn't wait around for the frog to show itself. Instead, it rushes once again up a spruce, dissolving in the dense cover of spruce needles. Moments later it chatters, informing an intruder that it is aware of its presence. Below the spruce branches has wandered a moose. Bears, wolves, moose are the iconic animals of the northern forest, and the largest of them all now stands below the red squirrel.

The young bull pulls on a young birch, stripping the leaves, then another, before moving on toward the river, stopping every few steps to listen and feed. It's mid-summer, and the bull has regained the strength lost during winter, gaining weight like a fuel drum at the pump. At this time of year, and in its current physical condition, the moose can handle its adversaries in the forest—bears and wolves. All except *Homo sapiens*, of course, but hunting is several weeks away, so its odds of getting shot are slim, and here, far beyond the end of the road, if it stays away from the river's edge and under the nearly impermeable canopy of branches and leaves, it won't be seen by river-hunters or the well-armed air force of small float planes circling overhead looking for a flash of antlers and a nearby small lake on which to land.

At the river's edge, willows form a cue, and the moose devours the leaves before sliding into the river seeking relief from the mosquitoes and increasing number of horseflies. It dips its head and splashes water cross its back.

Above the moose, in the branches of a spruce, a grouse watches. A remarkable and beautiful bird that flourishes in the boreal forest, this one, a male, is alone but will soon be joined by a group of females who seem to barely tolerate him but who will eventually mate and keep the population alive and well. In the fall, particularly throughout September, spruce grouse seem everywhere.

In our cabin yard we are often joined in the mornings by a group that varies between four and twelve, one of them a dominant male strutting continuously among the females, cornering one at a time, until she flies away a short distance. The male puffs up its face and fans its tail feathers, marching as fancy as any palace guard. When we walk between the buildings at our place, we weave among the birds. They scurry along and we step aside to give them room.

Never to be confused with graceful, when they fly, grouse resemble an airbus; when they land, it's a controlled crash. Or mostly controlled, for when they land on the cabin roof in the early mornings, we often spring from the bed expecting to see a bear has bounded upon our deck. Usually about noon they disappear from the yard for the day, although they can be flushed from both the ground and trees by a walk in the nearby woods.

Owls eat spruce grouse, and they sometimes patrol the edge of the clearing at the homestead. Both great horned and great gray owls live in the vicinity, though rarely seen because they are crepuscular and nocturnal.

Let's imagine a massive great gray owl, sitting on a birch branch extending beyond the river bank, disguised with leaves and intertwining branches, looks for food, perhaps because the night before had been unproductive. It's a carnivore and feeds on mostly small rodents, from tiny mice to rabbits, but will also eat fish, birds, and frogs. Unlike eagles, large birds that stay clear of entanglements with branches, the owl will hunt in the trees, flying within them, maneuvering tight spaces. The curvature and motion of their wings are unmistakable.

Great gray owls eat beavers, and one of those, its anvil head level with its rear end which is level with its tail, pulls a leafy branch below the owl in the river. What a conflict it must be for nocturnal animals to hunt during the day. The owl hesitates. It can get eaten, too, but as a fully grown raptor, its risk of becoming another animal's meal is low unless it is injured. The carnivores and omnivores of the forest, even the diminutive red squirrel, will eat an owl if the opportunity arises.

The owl evaluates the swimming beaver and passes. The beaver, the largest rodent in North America, claws its way up a worn pathway onto dry ground, perhaps unaware it was being considered for dinner.

The beaver resides in a hut on a small pond fifty feet off the river. Before it begins the arduous pull over land to the hut, it stands and curls its front legs before its chest much like a red squirrel does and seems to smile with orange front choppers.

These incisors get their orange color from the iron in the enamel covering their teeth. Beavers must chisel and chew away at trees—here mostly birch—or their incisors will grow until they are no longer useful and the beaver dies; the same thing will happen to a red squirrel if it is unable to chew. We see the results of beavers tending to their teeth all along our lengthy river trip to the homestead—beautiful, some quite large, birch chopped down along the river's edge. Near the cabin we retrieve these trees for firewood.

The beaver is swarmed by mosquitoes, which is not a surprise because it has helped create the ideal environment for the kamikaze aviators of the boreal forest. Mosquitoes develop in water, the more motionless the better, and beavers are masters at adapting its place to contain pools of stagnant water. Mosquitoes at times cloud the sky at our homestead, and beavers deserve some of the credit, or blame, depending on what's judging. To the dragonfly, it's a good thing.

Dragonflies appear in late May, and by the middle of summer they reach a length of five inches or so and are among the fastest flying creatures on earth. I've witnessed a dragonfly launch from Doylanne's knee to grab a mosquito in midflight and immediately return to her knee to enjoys its lunch—zip and back. A remarkable characteristic of dragonflies is that they seem to like people. Dragonflies treat Doylanne as the mother ship, resting on her shoulders, arms, and legs for long stretches and sometimes in her hair, creating a lovely, sometimes red, sometimes blue, sometimes green iridescent pin like no other.

The dragonfly has its predators too, of course. Birds flutter and glide across the yard and through the trees during all but the stormiest days, when apparently, they just stay home like we do. Juncos, thrushes, boreal chickadees, American robins, and gray jays are the most common birds in the area, although downy woodpeckers are frequent musicians in the trees. They all feast on dragonflies, as do spiders and frogs and ducks and fish.

Three fish species reside here year around, although there is a modest salmon run that amounts to a few out-of-place, worn-out monsters hundreds of miles from the Bering Sea where they enter and travel the Yukon and three other rivers to reach our place.

The locals are Arctic grayling, Northern pike, and burbot. Grayling spread through the river, pike congregate at the mouths of streams and deeper pools near the mouth of the river, as do burbot. All are edible, some might say delicious. I suppose that's what their natural predators conclude. River otters and eagles prefer fish but will eat whatever presents itself, but osprey, lightning fast and scary raptors, eat only fish.

Down river, just a turn, an osprey nest has been occupied the past dozen years or so. The nest, placed on top of a spruce at the edge of the river, provides a viewing area for a straight half mile reach of river. The pair are there when we arrive in May. They behave differently than eagles when they see us coming. Eagles stay put in the nest or on the branch where they are perched. They watch but don't react. Osprey, however, immediately take flight, circling and sounding a high, shrill squeak. Later, when tending to eggs or newly hatched chicks, only one will depart to chase us away. Both eagles and osprey leave the river by late September.

We spend a lot of our time in the woods interacting with animals. Sometimes it's from afar as when swans pass near; or it's much too close, like when a black bear stops to look in a window.

We cherish those times, the moments when Doylanne aims her camera at a wild animal. I feel the excitement too. Wilderness is required for this because it is only when we venture beyond our normal paths that we can observe and appreciate wild creatures in their homes and, by doing so, recognize how we are all connected.

We are, after all, animals too.

On September 23, the main squirrel from the midden behind the guest cabin pulled on a cord I had tied to a woodshed corner post. I couldn't remember why it was there, dangling from the post. Again, Doylanne saw it first. I crept closer, as she did for photographs, and the squirrel saw us but didn't stop pulling. The cord fell loose from its jaws and the grip of its paws several times, but it stayed persistent—jerking, rearing backward, and twisting. Was it playing? I was reminded of our small dog Rocky, buried just yards away from the woodshed near the river. Rocky, a toy poodle only three pounds fully grown—a giant compared to the squirrel—would have reacted to this cord the same way as the squirrel, pulling and shapping. The squirrel kept at it for perhaps a couple minutes, which is a long time for a wild animal to stay put, and we closed the gap to three feet four inches before the squirrel was struck with better sense and ran away.

# NINE

# SQUIRRELS AS EXPLORERS & SCIENTISTS

*If any person thinks the examination of the rest
of the animal kingdom an unworthy task, he must
hold in like disesteem the study of man.*

—Aristotle, *The History of Animals*

I learned a few things while attempting to replicate Emma's study. First, a red squirrel can ascend to royalty in the boreal forest. Main squirrels are monarchs of an acre, rulers of a castle. They weigh nine ounces yet prosper in one of the harshest environments on earth where temperatures drop to -70 degrees Fahrenheit. They are surrounded by predators, including their own species, who would gratefully eat them. Life is short by *Homo sapiens* standards but not out of line for other animals in the region. They utilize an economic philosophy that is taught to humans at the finest universities: work, save, and diversify. They're clean, well-groomed, and fit, always ready to move at lightning speed. They are handsome, funny, and brave. They defend against some predators by signaling, "I'm here. Come and get me." They can live most anywhere and sometimes venture where they can't.

Red squirrels inhabit a wide range that circles the earth. Follow a band between the 45th and 70th parallels, and you will encounter lots of red squirrels. Our homestead rests on the 64th.

Ruffed grouse and spruce grouse—lovely birds
that like to take over the yard.

Sometimes they venture outside that wide swath. Jon Holmgren, machinist and explorer, shared this story with me about a squirrel he encountered far north of its normal range:

> I was working on the North Slope of the Brooks Range a few years back doing snow research. We had a research site on Imnaviat Creek not far from Toolik Lake. On this particular occasion we had left Fairbanks in the dead of winter to check our snow thermal monitoring station to make sure that the foxes had not chewed on the data logger wires and that the battery had not frozen solid. We had several days of measuring and recording snow data ahead of us. On site was an old 1950s copy of an Airstream trailer that was to be our home and shelter from the elements. We left town with the Major and Sargent from our office at the Corps of Engineers. They wanted to see exactly what we did in the field on these trips. After driving all day, it was pitch black when we let ourselves through the pipeline gate and parked the trucks and started to unload the snowmobiles for the mile or two trip to the trailer. We loaded up and proceeded through the wind and blowing snow to find the snow drifts were about halfway up the walls and had completely blocked the door. After shoveling and hacking the door free, we opened it to find the drift

half filling the insides of the trailer as well. The Major and Sargent were a little dismayed that this was the cozy shelter from the elements that we had so glowingly described. After another half hour of heaving snow out the door and getting the big propane burner to light, we were almost ready to relax after a long day.

All of a sudden, out of the back room of the trailer came a whirlwind of motion, bouncing from one wall to the other came a red squirrel on a frantic dash for the still open door. Out he went into the cold night before we really knew what had happened.

Beavers look serious when swimming but happy on the shore.

We questioned what a red squirrel was doing so far north of his normal range and how he had gotten there and survived so long. On opening the cupboards the only food we found that he had eaten was a two pound bag of whole coffee beans that was completely hollowed out. It must have been a surreal experience for

A raptor that hunts within the trees.

him as it was for us. Sadly, we found him frozen in a pipe under the trailer the next morning.

This little guy might have been the farthest north red squirrel in Alaska, a true pioneer and explorer.

I admired squirrels long before this investigation, and as I learned more about them, my appreciation grew. As one of the most ubiquitous and accessible mammals on earth, it's safe to speculate that its influence on mankind has been significant. Like a rainbow or a cumulus cloud, or a tree bowing before the wind itself, squirrels can stop us in our tracks for a look. We pause and wonder. Imagine.

Imagine a fat red squirrel lives in the lush English countryside in the year 1667. It sprints across a garden to a larch and instantly ascends the conifer to the top. It now has a view of Woolsthorpe Manor in Lincolnshire near Grantham. A rainbow with magnificent colors and clarity arches over the manor house. Isaac Newton, feeling a bit better after days of melancholy, approaches with his field book, wiping the last drops of falling rain from his head, observing the rainbow and jotting notes.

Overhead a peregrine falcon circles, so the squirrel weaves down the tree, deeper into the needles for more cover. The falcon swoops near the larch and the frightened squirrel leaps to an apple tree and misses, falling like an over-ripe cranberry from a stem. The falcon disappears in the tall russet grass in an adjacent field. The squirrel, stunned, lies motionless for a few moments as Isaac steps lightly toward it. At three feet, four inches, it darts up the apple tree.

The young college student moves under the Flower of Kent and looks up through the dense leaves as the

Swans often run the river with us.

squirrel picks a small green cooking apple with a reddish hue and drops it. Isaac slumps to the ground holding his head before turning to his notebook, feverishly writing. For several minutes he alternates between writing and touching the growing knot on his forehead. He hears a noise in front of him.

The small squirrel, now on the ground, holds an apple in her hands. She steps a few feet closer.

"Do you get it now?" she asks.

I imagine it could have happened that way.

A rainbow is a refraction of white light.

# TEN

# WHAT CAN WE LEARN?

*Most people would succeed in small things if they*
*were not troubled with great ambitions.*

—Henry Wadsworth Longfellow, "Table Talk," *Driftwood*

On to the point of the study and results:

After watching squirrels intently during a month in the spring and a month in the fall, I've altered my view of their place among the animals in the boreal forest. I've seen no evidence that squirrels idolize larger animals or fear them, for that matter. Squirrels don't gather and bow to bears or wolves. They stand their own and control their mini kingdoms, often standing in plain sight enjoying a meal of fresh spruce seeds. Certainly a mistake can mean their end, but that's true for all animals. Squirrels, at a prudent distance, notify intruders that they have invaded their space. That is not subservient behavior.

We all can be kings and queens if we care to be. We just have to be realistic about the size and scope of our kingdom. Yes, squirrels are monarchs of an acre in the wilderness, and so can we be if we realistically define the boundaries of our province. Perhaps our domain is a garden, a reading chair, park bench, small business, or family. I believe many of us struggle with this notion, though, because we believe kingdoms must be big and can only belong to a few. It's no surprise that we hold these beliefs because that is what we are taught and what those in power want us to accept. We must not, after all, become too proud or independent. This fixation and idealization of powerful people is a cause for the messy world we live in today. The natural world offers a different story and a different way.

•

I've described the landscape of our homestead without identifying its specific location. It's not necessary to do that and generally not a wise thing to do. The squirrels described here are wild and live near the center of the state of Alaska, where the average low temperature in January in this locale is -13 degrees Fahrenheit but can reach -70. The average high in July is 72 degrees but can fluctuate 20 degrees either way. The land is rolling hills with white and black spruce forests and vast expanses of swamps and meadows. There are more bears and moose then people, more old people than young people, more black bears than grizzlies. Mosquitoes can change a day and a mind. There are no roads in this area. The few trails that exist are only passable in the winter, and that's only by skilled and experienced travelers with the right equipment. Most travel is done by airplane on skis and floats. Some, as we do, pass through the land via shallow rivers that change as quickly as thoughts. Mistakes are not treated well and consequences can be dire. That's where this study was conducted.

Spruce cones for squirrel bait.

I hypothesized that red squirrels would demonstrate more diligence and less boldness than the squirrels in a population of Eastern gray squirrels in the Boston Common Central Burying Ground. I compared my findings with a study done in 2019 by Emma Rademacher, a college student at Boston University. To test diligence and boldness, I attempted to replicate the methodology used by Emma. To test vigilance, I measured flight initiation distance (FID). To test boldness, I recorded the time it took for each squirrel to obtain a spruce cone from me. My results supported my hypotheses.

I thought squirrels would be easy to find, observe, and test;

however, in May and early June, they didn't present themselves as I expected. In a month, I saw three squirrels. In September, when I returned to the homestead, the activity seemed normal, but I realized that I was seeing the same squirrel multiple times. Although I had a sizeable number of sightings, I only saw three different squirrels. As well, the single squirrel I saw the most often, may have begun changing its behavior over time, becoming less vigilant as it became accustomed to me.

Red squirrels like high, open places to eat.

For the boldness and the vigilance parts of the study. I used spruce cones instead of nuts because there aren't nuts in the area. Not a single squirrel even came close to taking a cone from my hand. I sat often under trees with squirrels overhead, sweeping away mosquitoes (which was likely a limitation as well) but seeing no squirrel activity. Squirrels, however, did take cones from our cabin deck. I placed ten cones on the deck in a location not far from the front door, and the number of cones diminished by two or three each night. I didn't write down the data to verify the rate. Of course, a cabin deck is not a hand.

An area worthy of more investigation is whether or not the study methods themselves train squirrels to become less vigilant and less bold. As mentioned before, that issue began to bother me as September went on and I was able to get closer to the squirrel that lived in the main midden. I assumed that the squirrel learned from my behavior—a big mammal inching toward it—that I was not a danger to it. That might not be a good thing for the squirrel to learn.

What are the behavioral differences between spring and autumn? As said earlier, I was surprised that there weren't more squirrels running about in May and June. I speculated the reason was related to birthing and nesting. Maybe. Maybe not. More study is needed.

The outcomes of the inquiry are on the following pages:

**Figure 1: Eric Wade's Vigilance Study Results
from May 2022 through September 2022**

| Date | Location | FID (feet) | Comments |
|------|----------|-----------|----------|

**June 2** **Deck steps** **11** Brilliant day, the screen
densely dotted with mosquitoes attempting to gain entry.
Doylanne saw it at the bottom of the deck steps. I walked slowly
toward the squirrel, and it darted away.

**June 2** **Woodshed** **13** It froze for a few moments
watching me, and when I moved, it sprinted off, its first steps
toward me, then veered into the woods.

**June 12** **Woodshed** **8** It sprang away with a
mouthful of cardboard. I was surprised when it returned while I
measured the distance. It didn't stay, but it rapidly ran by me, up
the wood pile, and away, disappearing in the brush.

**Sept 8** **Back yard** **22** The squirrel stopped on
en it saw me but immediately went back to eating. I stepped slowly
and as softly as I could but didn't get close.

**Sept 9** **Base of spruce** **9** It circled the tree several
times then came to rest on the ground and began gnawing on a
cone. I watched this squirrel all day. It ran up the tree and jumped
between branches, always returning to the base of the spruce tree.

**Sept 11** **Deck steps** **4** The squirrel was
surrounded by cone scales, indicating it had been there for some
time. It ran into the tall grass at the river's edge.

**Sept 12** **Central midden** **9** Near the central midden
north of the cabin, the main squirrel and I faced off for several
minutes before I began my advance. This squirrel, the monarch of
the midden behind the guest cabin, was likely becoming familiar
with Doylanne and me.

**Sept 17** **Near central midden** **10** With a gigantic mushroom in its mouth, it sat on the bottom branch of a spruce, about eye height for me, frozen. I approached the squirrel, slowly, until it dashed away, scampering to the ground and over the midden to another nearby spruce, springing to a branch and disappearing in the evergreen.

**Sept 20   Woodshed                3        The squirrel saw me** coming but didn't react. It stopped chewing once but didn't move. I stepped closer and closer until I could clearly see its whiskers. I slowly extended an empty hand, palm up, wondering. It then darted.

**Sept 21   Woodshed                6        The same squirrel in the** same spot.

**Sept 21   Upriver milling site   20        In the evening when the first** hints of twilight settled on the land, upriver a quarter mile where I made boards from a wind-blown spruce with a chainsaw mill, a new squirrel became an entry. This one wasn't having much of it.

**Sept 23   Woodshed                3        The squirrel saw us but did** not stop pulling on a cord tied to a post in the woodshed. The cord fell loose from its jaws and the grip of it paws several times, but it stayed persistent, jerking, rearing backward, and twisting.

The average FID in the spring was 10.6 feet; 9.5 feet in the fall. The first encounters always resulted in a greater FID, so the meeting with a new squirrel on September 21 should be noted. Without that data point, the fall FID was 8.2 feet. I didn't get too close to the squirrels at the homestead compared to Emma's experiences.

**Figure 2: Eric Wade's Boldness Study Results from May 2022 through September 2022**

No results! Zero! In eight weeks, I was unable to entice a squirrel to take a cone from my hand.

Interior of our little cabin. Note our reflection in the window.

# ANNOTATED BIBLIOGRAPHY

This tale includes the accumulated knowledge of most of a lifetime of traveling into the Alaska interior boreal forest, a vast and complex place. But as mentioned early in the book, I borrowed from many sources. Here are those most significant to me.

I must start with Barry Lopez. His *Of Wolves and Men* (New York, Charles Scribner's Sons, 1978), National Book Award finalist; *Arctic Dreams* (Scribner, 1986), National Book Award winner; and *Horizon* (Knopf, 2019) are among the best natural history books ever written. All three—but particularly *Of Wolves and Men*—influenced this book. I attempted Lopez's approach to "imagine" the movements and activities of a wild animal.

Richard K. Nelson's *Make Prayers to the Raven* (University of Chicago Press, 1983), among the best books about the Koyukon people of northcentral Alaska, provided insight on the cultural importance of the squirrel in the northland, but his influence extends further because I consider him one of the most lyrical voices of the north.

Nunakun-gguq Ciutengqertut, *They Say They Have Ears Through the Ground: Animal Essays from Southwest Alaska*, edited by Ann Fienup-Riordan with Alice Rearden, et al (University of Alaska Press, 2020), describes Yup'ik beliefs and understandings of animals in southwest Alaska. This is an academic book that is eminently readable and entertaining.

Velma Wallis's *Raising Ourselves*, (Epicenter Press, 2003), a moving account of growing up in the wilds of the far northern boreal forest, made me think about the restorative power of the

Lowbush cranberries—bear love them.

Blueberries—bear love these too.

wilderness.

For information about squirrels, I leaned heavily on Michael A. Steele's and John L. Koprowski's *North American Tree Squirrels* (Smithsonian Institution Press, 2001) and Richard Thorington Jr and Katie Ferrell's *Squirrels: The Animal Answer Guide* (Johns Hopkins University Press, 2006). Both books are squirrel encyclopedias, describing squirrels in ways easy to see and understand. I also enjoyed

Kim Long's natural history titled *Squirrels: A Wildlife Handbook* (Johnson Books, 1995), a book that starts with tales and myths and becomes a resource guide for just about everything squirrel related. Anchorage based nature writer Bill Sherwonit's *Animal Stories: Encounters with Alaska's Wildlife* (Alaska Northwest Books, 2014) provided information about red squirrels and wood frogs that I found useful. Paul Vincent Krasnowski's master's thesis *Aspects of Red Squirrel (Tamiasciurus hudsonicus) Population Ecology in Interior Alaska* (Fairbanks, University of Alaska, 1969) was fascinating, and I discuss his work in the text, but I suspect his research methods might be controversial today; many of his research subjects were shot in order to collect data.

A theme in the book is the exaggerated admiration for size and power in our society. This is an old notion, but I was struck by Yuval Noah Harari's take on the topic in *Sapiens: A Brief History of Humankind* (HarperCollins, 2015), Heather Cox's article "The Cowboy Mythology: Twenty Years Since the Reagan Revolution and the Rise of Movement Conservatives" (*Milwaukee Independent*, Jan. 31, 2021), and James Plath's "Shadow Rider: The Hemingway Hero as Western Archetype" (*Hemingway and the Natural World*, Robert E. Fleming, ed., 1999).

Two other titles of importance to this book are Victor Van Ballenberghe's *In the Company of Moose* (Stackpole Books, 2004), a beautifully written, personal account of decades studying moose, and Gavin Pretor-Pinny's *The Cloudspotter's Guide* (Hodder and Stoughton, 2006), a must read for anyone who looks to the sky for inspiration and guidance.

I began each chapter with an epigraph. I have read each of the works I borrowed from, and they all meant something important to me. Perhaps the one that resonates most at this time begins chapter five: William Least Heat-Moon's "Getting what we know to dawn on us is a fundamental human bugaboo."

The major fiction references were included in the text, so I won't repeat them here.

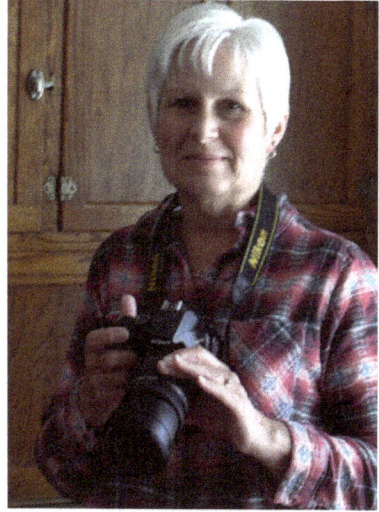

ERIC WADE, author of *Upstream: In the Alaska Wilderness* and *Cabin: An Alaska Wilderness Dream*, has spent the past four decades watching and dodging wildlife on his homestead in interior Alaska. It's a wild and lovely place where bears wander by, eagles soar overhead, squirrels build kingdoms, and mosquitos engage in savage warfare. He has a bachelor's degree in English education from Southern Oregon University and a master's in journalism from the University of Oregon. He served as a public-school teacher, principal, and director of nonprofit corporations.

DOYLANNE WADE has long told wilderness stories with her camera. Lady bugs, dragonflies, bumble bees, and ants; foxes, gray wolves, black bears, and lynx have all been captured with her camera in her more than forty years in Alaska. She has a special appreciation for the small creatures that mostly go unnoticed in a vast and majestic landscape. She now uses a DSLR camera with 150–600mm and 18–270 lenses.

# Shanti Arts

## Nature · Art · Spirit

Please visit us online
to browse our entire book catalog,
including poetry collections and fiction,
books on travel, nature, healing, art,
photography, and more.

Also take a look at our highly regarded art
and literary journal, *Still Point Arts Quarterly*,
which may be downloaded for free.

www.shantiarts.com